I'm Grateful for You